RHYMING IT UP WITH CHURCH STUFF

RHYMING IT UP WITH CHURCH STUFF

JUANITA TRAVIS

J MERRILL

J MERRILL

For permission requests, please contact the Permissions Coordinator at:

J Merrill Publishing, Inc.
434 Hillpine Drive
Columbus, OH 43207
www.JMerrill.pub

Paperback ISBN-13: *978-1-961475-43-4*
eBook ISBN-13: *978-1-961475-44-1*

Book Title: *Rhyming It Up with Church Stuff*
Author: *Juanita Travis*

*I dedicate this book to the members of **New Jerusalem Missionary Baptist Church.***

*A special thank-you to **Pastor Martin** for allowing me to express my love of God to the congregation through my poetry.*

TABLE OF POEMS

CHAPTER 1
WALK CAUTIOUSLY

As we grow in our Christian life,
We must do what's pleasing in God's sight.

I know what He's asking of me,
So I'm going to walk cautiously.

We have to crawl before we walk,
But remember, as we crawl, the devil will stalk.

He's there to lure you when you're most weak,
Just ask God for strength and walk cautiously.

I've learned to pray for others as well as myself,
I know God is the source of all our help.

To our church, let's give generously—

We must support our church in ministry.
Always help financially; when we give, do it
cheerfully.

Let's give more of ourselves—there's so much to
share,
Aid the sick and distressed, show them we care.

If there's someone whose words did not spare,
Try to forgive them and lift them up in prayer.

We must show our love for one another,
Give thanks for our sisters and brothers.

Let us stand together in Christian love—
It's a promise to our Lord above.

I'm going to try and do my very best,
I know if I do, I'll surely be blessed.

I'll let God guide my steps for me,
And I shall continue to walk cautiously.

CHAPTER 2
THE ROAD TO HEAVEN

You might say the road to heaven is kind of
rough,
Well, not so hard if in the Lord you trust.

What's important is the choices you make,
And you have to be careful of the roads you take.

If you take the roads of gossip and lies,
You're in for a big head-on collision—no surprise.
And it will run you right down into the road of
despair,
And you don't want to wind up there.

Because around the bend, there's a fork in the
road,
And you have to decide which way to go.

Go either way if you might,
But when you do, make sure you're doing what's
right.

Now don't go too fast and wind up crashing—
You just might miss the road of compassion.

See, it's going to keep you in a straight and
narrow lane.
Don't you mind running into a little rain.

Into each life, some rain must fall,
But you don't have to worry about that at all.

Because the Lord is with you, and He will take
care.
He knows how much you can bear.

Listen, stay away from the valley of hate.
Just keep on moving—keep going straight.

Now, if you happen to find yourself heading to
the road of sadness,
Just take the overpass to joy and gladness.

There's a highway up above,
And it's going to run you smack dab into the road
of love.

Now you're on your way—you're heaven bound.
You've come too far, so don't turn around.

You might see the road of darkness—
Don't go that way; it will steer you off course and
lead you astray.

So, like I said, keep going straight and let your
light shine.
Keep the Lord Jesus on your mind.

And lo and behold, you're gonna see the highway
of faith—
Then you're surely down for those pearly gates.

CHAPTER 3
ONE BIG BODY OF CHRIST

Sometimes the shoulders carry a very heavy load.
It's the head—it doesn't know which way to go.

It'll throw the whole body off-key,
With those wide eyes trying to see
What's all wrong with you and me.

And the ears sometimes don't hear,
But negativity comes in loud and clear.

Shut up, tongue—you're the worst yet,
Taking in all the gossip you can get.

The left hand won't let the right know what's
going on.
They have to come together and be strong.

No wonder the shoulders are so stressed and
strained—
There's nothing going on up there in the brain.

It's got to think and take the lead,
Then other parts will take heed.

Don't let the feet go astray,
All mixed up, going every which way.

Let the Lord guide them each day,
Then they'll walk the righteous way.

Get that head screwed on right.
Focus those eyes for better insight.

Tongue, get on one accord—
Use yourself to praise the Lord.

The Word—you should listen, ears—
That's what's important for you to hear.

Let's all get on a path that's right
And work together as one big Body of Christ.

CHAPTER 4
PRAY FOR ME

Can't make service today, Sis Sue—
Gotta heap of things I needs to do.
Mayhap next week, we'll see.
Tell Rev. Pastor, **pray for me.**

Sorry 'bout Bible study,
Me not getting out.
What's them lessons about?
Be there mayhap next week, we'll see.
Tell Rev. Pastor, **pray for me.**

'Tis a shame—
Couldn't make service today.
Heard tell Reverend had a heap to say.
Well, mayhap next Sunday, we'll see.
Tell Rev. Pastor, **pray for me.**

Can't make service—
Got folk coming to town.
They be tired, I gots to bed 'em down.
Probably might next week, we'll see.
Tell Rev. Pastor, **pray for me.**

You know, tomorrow I'm havin' a big ol' feast—
Gots to mix my rolls and fix my meats.
Ain't gonna make service tonight,
Gotta see to it everything's right.
Mayhap next Sunday, we'll see.
Tell Rev. Pastor, **pray for me.**

Whoooie! Up late last night—
Needs my rest—
Ain't gonna make service, I don't guess.
Mayhap next week, we'll see.
Tell Rev. Pastor, **pray for me.**

Here of late, feelin' kinda low,
Just don't have no get-up-and-go.
This ol' body ain't worth two cents—
Feels like my get-up done got up and went.

I feel so worn out and beat,
Just plain tired, and I feel weak.
Try to take care of this and such,
These days, I can't do much.

Seems like everybody's goin' wrong.
I'm gonna come to service—it won't be long.
Mayhap next week, we'll see.
Tell Rev. Pastor, **pray for me.**

Tell me, how's ol' Sis Kate?
She ain't called here of late.
Last she did, I ain't had time—
Had a heap of things on my mind.

Ain't seen my friends, not even my kin.
Ain't nobody been stoppin' in.
You still singin' in the choir, Sis Sue?
Anybody took my place on the pew?

You know I'd come to service if I could.
If I could, I surely would.
Miss hearin' Rev. Pastor speak—
That man sure 'nuff can preach!

Bro. Jones still drivin' that ol' church bus?
Reckon he'd swing 'round and pick me up?
I gets up early as the birds in the trees,
Ain't gonna have to wait on me.

I'll be ready right on time—
Ain't gonna let nothin' change my mind. *(hum)*

Sho' is a beautiful Sunday morn.
I best step it up, 'cause sho' as I'm born,
Bro. Jones be swingin' 'round, blowin' that horn,
And I ain't missin' service—uh-uh, no way!

I sho' gonna make it to church today!

Mornin', Sis Kate!
Mornin', Bro. Brown!
Mornin', Sis Sue!
Sho' feels good here with my church family—
We all here amongst one another.
I sho' did miss my sisters and brothers.

Bro. Jones, be sure and swing 'round with
that bus—
I be ready for you to pick me up!

Rev. Pastor, I sho' enjoyed the sermon you
preached.
I'm gonna be here come next week!

Oh yes, sho' gonna be here—you'll see.
I'll pray for y'all, y'all **pray for me.** (*hum*)

CHAPTER 5
SIS MAGGIE & HER SENIOR CHOIR – PART I

DEDICATED TO WILMA J. CAROLINA

Good morning, Sis Sally, Sis Sue, Bro. Gray.
How is everybody doing today?

Come on in, have a seat,
I have just a few words whilst we meet.

Now first thing—we gotta work on our sway.
Y'all be swingin' every which way!

And before we start, I just want to say—
Y'all s'posed to sing, and I s'posed to play.

Now let's head on up to the choir stand.
Brother Brown gonna give you ladies a hand.

Bless his heart, he tries to help,
But he can barely make it up them steps himself!

I hope we get through this rehearsal without
delay,
'Cause they s'posed to sing, and I s'posed to play.

And now, I got the pitch horn to give y'all the key.
Y'all keep your eyes focused on me.

Oh Lord, I better play somethin' upbeat—
'Fore Sis Sally done gone to sleep!

Okay, let's go—
"Glory, Glory, Hallelujah!"

Hold it! Hold it! Didn't I just give y'all the note?
Y'all sound like you got a bunch of frogs in your
throat!

Lord, just show me the way.
They s'posed to sing, and I s'posed to play.

I tried to give them the pitch—
Whew! They 'bout to give me a fit!

So now everybody got their part.
Okay, so I guess we're ready to start.

Okay, we're gonna go left to right, left to right—
We don't wanna be here all night!

All right, let's take it right from the top.
Just keep on goin'—don't y'all stop.

Now stay on key, and let me see that sway,
Because y'all s'posed to sing, and I s'posed to
play.

Listen, y'all in the back row—
Y'all stompin' so hard you sound like a herd of
buffalo!

Now we're gonna march out two by two—
Don't y'all be tryin' to do the Boogaloo!

Stay in line as y'all prance—
Go head on, y'all, do your dance.

Lord, I thank You for lettin' us get a little practice
in.
Be Your will, we'll meet again.

And Lord, also as I pray—
Just let them know, they s'posed to sing, and I
s'posed to play.

CHAPTER 6
SIS MAGGIE & HER SENIOR CHOIR – PART II

Listen up, y'all—it's almost time
For our annual Music Jubilee!

Sing a song now, *"Good Night."*
We wanna be the best that we can be.

This is our last rehearsal tonight,
So we wanna be sure to get it right.

I can't believe that time is almost here—
Sure hope there's no mishaps this year.

Yes, we had a few glitches on the way,
But through it all, we had a blessed day.

Now y'all gotta remember to get in the
right row—
Sis Agnes sang soprano, but wound up singin'
alto!

Y'all, bless his heart—
I wondered why Bro. Brown was stumblin' to his
seat,
Looked down—his shoes was on the wrong feet!

Lord, y'all hear Sis Higgins stoppin' to chit-chat?
Ain't nobody got time for that!
I'm tryin' to get everybody together,
And she runnin' her mouth about the weather!

Y'all, we missed Sis Sally—
Wondered where she at.
Found her on the back pews takin' a nap!

Y'all, I just stopped and prayed.
I said, *Lord, I'm truly tryin' to serve,*
But these folks 'bout to get on my last nerve!

Yes sir, we had some glitches on the way,
But yet and still, we had a blessed day.

(Hee hee!) Y'all remember when Sis Bradshaw
Was struttin' down the aisle?

Y'all know how she love to style!
Well, she tripped and fell,
Lost her hat,
And her wig came flyin' off right after that!

Now, now—she didn't hurt herself,
Just her pride more than anything else.

Yes, it was some kind of sight!
Thank the Lord she was all right.

Maybe next time, she'll watch how she strut
through that door—
She don't wanna repeat pickin' herself up off the
floor!

Yes, there sho' nuff was some mishaps on the way,
But through it all, we had a blessed day.

Okay, y'all, just a few words before we start—
We need to work on our march.

Now y'all got that swingin' way,
But now y'all steppin' every which way!

Now watch—
We gonna step to the left and step to the right,
Step to the left and step to the right.

I ain't wantin' to stay here all night!

Listen, listen—
Samuella, set your alarm, for heaven's sake!
I don't know why these young folks always late!

Now, Samuella, you asked to sing with the
seniors, and I agreed—
But as I said, we have to be the best that we
can be!

It ain't fair for all of us havin' to wait,
Just 'cause you always runnin' late.

Runnin' in here—
Hair ain't combed,
Done left your music back at home!

And your lyrics take the cake—
Blamin' everybody else for your mistakes!

Now, Dougie Lee works and goes to school,
And he don't come runnin' in here late like you!

But now, all y'all, we gotta be on time—
Can't be knockin' folks down gettin' in line!

Bumpin' all into people in the row—

Folk be fallin' like dominoes!

I just wanna let y'all know—
We ain't goin' there for no show!

We all have to be on one accord,
Remember—we're there to praise and worship the
Lord!

Okay, we done went over the march step by
step—
Some of y'all ain't got it yet!

So we gonna walk up to our seat—
Y'all act like you got two left feet!

Now we gonna do a verse of this song—
So lift up your voices, we won't be long!

Sing loud—
Hold it! Hold it!

Where y'all think y'all at?
In a big ol' arena?
Y'all so loud,
You sound like a pack of hyenas!

When I say lift your voices and sing,

That don't mean for y'all to holla and scream!

Y'all gotta be ready to sing this song,
Just the way we practiced here at home.

Now, y'all, we gonna leave all the glitches and
mishaps behind,
We're gonna enjoy ourselves and have a good
time!

Lord, I thank You for our practice today.
There is one thing, as I pray—

Although last time, mishaps came our way,
I pray that we'll have a blessed day.

And Lord, one thing heavy on my mind—
Please let Samuella get herself there on time!

Amen.

CHAPTER 7
MIRROR TALK

Well, here we are—me and you.
I see everything you do.
'Cause I is you, and you is me,
And everything you do, I see.

First thing—grabbing that coffee cup,
Ain't thanked the Lord for waking you up!
If nothin' else, least you can just say,
"Thank You, Lord, for another day."

Why you staring at me?
I'm just your reflection—
We gonna always have a connection.
'Cause you see, we're two of a kind,
I also know what's on your mind.

Look at you, posing in your brand-new dress.
No money for tithes, I don't guess!
And you always tippin' in service late,
Talkin' 'bout, *"Oh, they already passed the plate."*
Even when you there on time,
Don't give nothin' but one thin dime!

Paid a heap more for that big ol' hat—
Now we know you can do better than that!
What hat, you asketh?
The one look like a big ol' laundry basket!

Uh-huh, I see them new shoes you done bought.
Did you thank the Lord? Even give Him a
thought?
I see everything you do—
'Cause you is me, and I is you.

Struttin' in the sanctuary, takin' a seat,
Nose in the air, can't even speak!
You can say *mornin'* to your sisters and brothers.
The Bible say we must love one another.

Ain't they fault your shoes too tight—
You knew that when you tried 'em on last night!

That's right—
Go on, change that dress.

You know that thing looks a hot mess!
Whilst you at it, change them shoes,
'Cause they sho' nuff ugly too.

Don't be havin' a fit, stompin' all about.
Better use that energy to praise and shout!
Don't get mad 'cause I see what you do—
Lord don't like ugly, He sees you too!

Stop all that pit-pattin' your hair,
And grab that Bible sittin' over there.
Fool around, get to service late,
Way after they done passed the plate!

Remember, don't hold back and pinch—
Make sure you give your ten percent!

Don't be noddin', for heaven's sake,
Try to keep yourself awake!
Bro. Pastor done preached and spoke,
And here you ain't even woke!

Done changed? That's nice!
Now twirl around and walk.
Ain't you glad we had this talk?

Go on now, be on your way.
Hurry it up, now—have a nice day!

Sometimes it's good to have a little conversation.
It just might be a little inspiration.
So while you on your Christian walk,
Won't hurt to have a little mirror talk.

So I guess the moral to my little story—
Do what sayeth the Lord,
If you wanna get to Glory!

CHAPTER 8
WE GON' HAVE A HI OLE TIME

Get up, y'all—
Brush your teeth and wash your face!
Gotta get to service, don't make me late!
'Cause come rain or shine,
I'm gonna have me a hi ole time!

I know Bro. Pastor got a good word today—
I ain't missin' it, uh-uh, no way!
There gonna be foot-stompin',
Hand-clappin',
And hands wavin' in the air—
Prancin' around like they just don't care!

Lil' Joe, you out there in the dirt—
Git in here and change your shirt!
Y'all out there goin' at it tit for tat,

Y'all don't want me to get my strap!

Git in here and put that basketball down!
I ain't got time to fool around.
Git in here, I say—and best hurry!
Y'all ain't no LeBron and Steph Curry!

Y'all keep it up, I'll leave you behind—
'Cause I'm gonna have me a hi ole time!

Ewe baby nose runnin'—
Grab that dish rag, Amy Sue!
Make sure you wipe it good too,
'Cause I despise nastiness, yes I do!

Hold it! Hold it! Leddy Mae,
Wait just a hot minute—
Where you fixin' to go in that getup?
Play some tennis?!

Ain't no tennis match where I fixin' to go!
Just march yourself up there and change those
clothes!

Ooh, done changed? That's nice!
You look just fine—
Now we gon' have a hi ole time!

Now look up there on that rack,
And hand me my big yella hat.
Grab my coat—let's be on our way,
We gonna have us a hi ole time today!

Oh Lord—
Here come Sis Talk-a-lot,
Showin' off her new teeth!

Hurry, Jr. Lee, hide my meat!
She comin' to do a heap of talkin'—
I ain't got time, I'm gonna keep on walkin'!

Soon as she spot my meat,
She be ready to take a seat.
She'll eat and eat and ask for more—
Hurry up, Jr., and close the door!

Oh Lord, too late—she done seen you!
Now she ain't hinderin' me,
I'm goin' anyhow!

Mornin', Sis Talk-a-lot—
(Sorry) Sis, Sis Out-a-lot—
(No, no) I'm sorry, Sis Lot More—
(No, no) Sis Greedy—
I'm sorry! I mean, Sis Bradshaw!

How you doin' today?
We about to be on our way.

You say you smell some smothered cabbage,
Yams, cornbread, and beef?
Yes ma'am, but we gotta go—
We don't have time to eat!

So we gon' be on our way.
Them some real nice teeth!
Yes ma'am, we'll talk to you soon—
Perhaps tomorrow afternoon!

Bye now—we gots to be on our way!
Them some nice teeth—
Have a blessed day!

Lawd, I thought she'd never leave!
Like I say, she ain't hinderin' me,
'Cause come rain or shine,
I'm gon' have me a hi ole time!

Lil' Joe, why you doin' all that fidgetin'?
Just stop it!

Leddy say it's 'cause you got
A piece of hot chicken in your pocket!

Put it back—
Before I knock yo' eyes outta socket!

Y'all ain't hinderin' me,
You hear what I say?
'Cause I'm havin' me a hi ole time today!

That ol' devil try to throw
All kinds of stumblin' stones—
He know what good for him,
He'll leave me alone! *(laughs)*

Now he think he can change my mind—
Ain't stoppin' me from havin' a hi ole time!

Now Lord, as I be on my way,
I thank You, Lord, for seein' another day.

I'm leavin' here with God on my mind,
'Cause He's the reason
I'm gonna have me a hi ole time!

Juanita Travis, 2024

ABOUT THE AUTHOR

Author Jaunita Travis was born in 1935, in Steubenville Ohio and grew up in Columbus Ohio where the values of faith, family, and community were deeply ingrained. Her Christian faith has been a guiding light throughout her life, influencing her worldview and her writing.

Juanita is blessed with a large and loving family. She and her late husband Daniel Travis have four children. Of those four children she has eleven grandchildren, and eighteen great-grandchildren. Her family has always been her greatest source of joy and inspiration, often finding their way into her poetry.

Juanita discovered her passion for poetry at a young age. Over the decades, she has penned numerous poems that reflect her faith, experiences, and the beauty of the world around her. Her work is celebrated for its heartfelt emotion and spiritual depth.

At 90 years old, Juanita continues to write, sharing her wisdom and faith through her poetry. Her legacy is not only in her written words but also in the love and values she has instilled in her family.

www.ingramcontent.com/pod-product-compliance
Lightning Source LLC
Chambersburg PA
CBHW031240120626
46545CB00003B/1206